LOST IN DREAMS AND SPATTERS OF LIGHT

Publisher, Copyright, and Additional Information

Lost in Dreams and Spatters of Light by Keith DeClerck

ISBNS:
979-8-9921766-3-6 (Paperback)

Editing by Spruce Spaulding
Cover design and interior design by Magnolia Theriot

LOST IN DREAMS
AND
SPATTERS OF LIGHT

A Collection of Poetry and Prose

Keith DeClerck

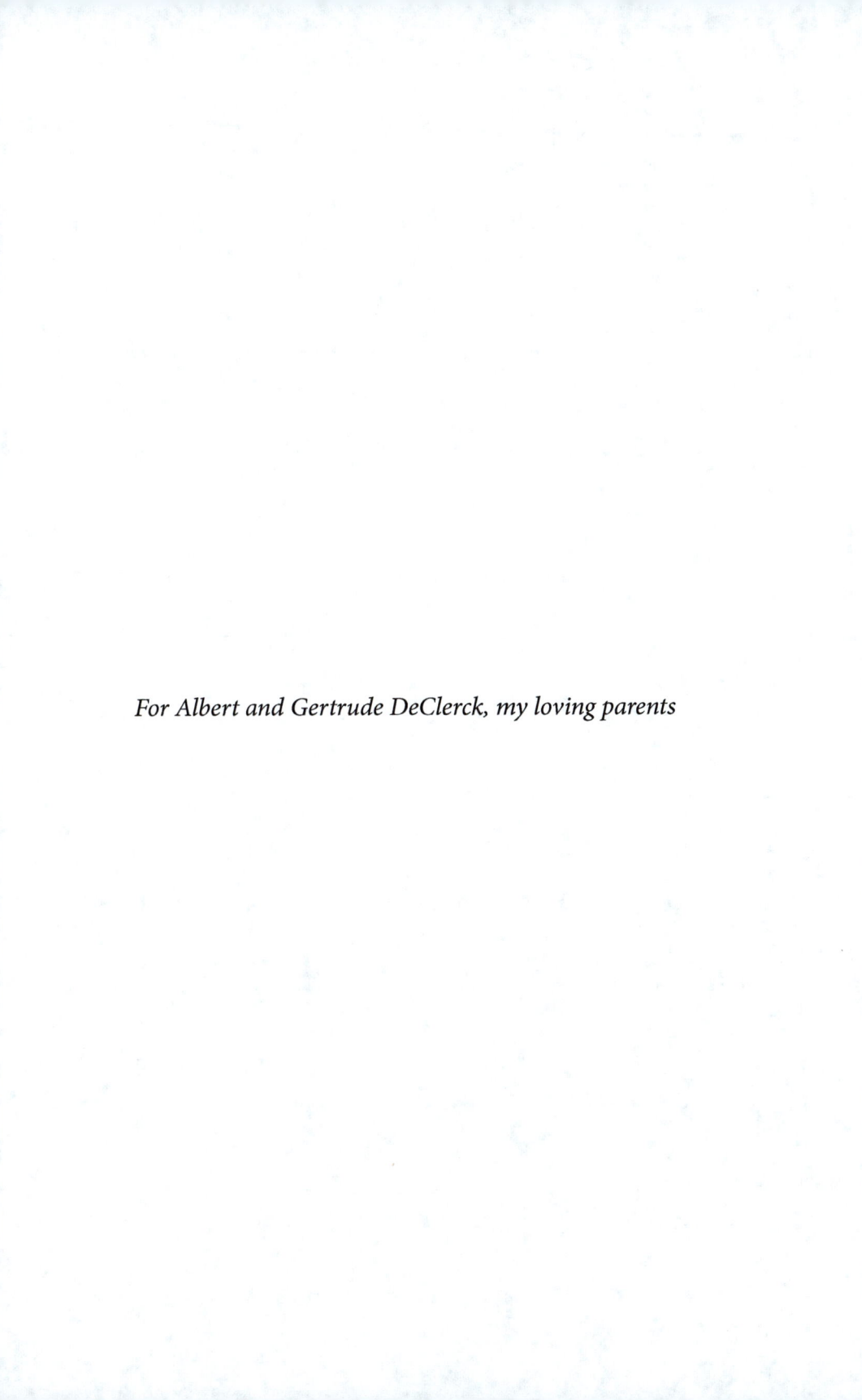

For Albert and Gertrude DeClerck, my loving parents

Acknowledgements

I want to thank LJP and Reality Ministries for making this collection of my work possible; and my wife, whom God placed in my life at a critical moment, as if an angel had been sent to block the furnace door

CONTENTS

TEACHER'S CAFÉ

Preface

While talking with Nicodemus, Jesus said, "For God so loved the world that He gave His only begotten Son, that whoever believes in Him should not perish but have everlasting life. For God did not send His Son into the world to condemn the world, but that the world *through Him* might be saved. John 3:16-17 (NKJV) (Italics added for emphasis.)

At the Last Supper, Thomas said to Him, "Lord, we do not know where You are going, and how can we know the way?" Jesus said to him, "I am the way, the truth, and the life. No one comes to the Father *except through Me.*" John 14:5-6 (NKJV) (Italics added for emphasis.)

In fiction, the author is god, and the story which follows gives John Michael McGee a second chance. In life, Jesus Christ is God, and He will judge according to his written Word. Those who believe in Him will not perish, but how can you believe in someone you've never known?

Teacher's Café - A Short Story

The ocean in all its vastness, dwarfing mountain ranges and plunging to immeasurable depths, has always been a source of inspiration and solace for me. The crashing surf, the salty mist, knowing that it is the source of wind and climate, acting as the fulcrum in a fragile balance of survival for all living creatures, allows me to reflect on the meager circumstance of humanity. Most of us, no matter our self-proclaimed importance or stature, are insignificant to the world. A sobering thought, which on these occasions would leave me to ponder: Where is the value in my life?

My name is John Michael McGee. My wife, Madeleine, and I own a place on the Oregon coast. Where exactly is not important, but what is important is the letter I found coiled into an empty glass bottle that floated ashore at my feet one day. When I first found the letter and the charred bottle that held it, I thought it might be a high school project to chart the tides and currents, or possibly the aching of a broken heart with nowhere else to turn. Yet as I opened the bottle, pulling the cork that was sealed over with a waxy mantel, I knew its contents would change my life, just as I knew the day our child was born that my journey had gained a greater purpose.

What follows now is the letter as I found it …

***

To whoever finds this letter, let me be your benefactor. For only hindsight sparkles with clarity, and that is all that I have to give.

When I arrived at the edge of the town, I stood in awe of its singular beauty. I could see the vein in every leaf of every tree that lined the street before me, the flesh of their trunks flickering in a golden light. The sky was a ceramic blue, as if a perfect teacup had been tipped over the world. How I had come to this place at first was a mystery. I had no recollection of a recent past; just a litany of flashes that defined my history, yet with each step, the truth became clearer, as if I was rising through a tent of bubbles to the surface of a crystalline lake.

This small town, which had no name I can recall, was much like the village in Vermont where my grandparents had lived when I was a child. Bungalows of white and blue and green stood back from the curb with friendly yards, the sprinklers of some casting out rainbows in the midday sun.

I walked toward what seemed in my mind as the center of town, although I did not know or care if I was strolling north or south, only sensing I was going the right direction, as though a migratory bird would make his journey without thought.

A knot of people stood at the corner as I approached, unnoticing at first, then welcoming me with a unified smile.

"Good day to you, sir," a dark-haired man said. "You look as though you have traveled far."

"Frankly, I do not know how far I have come."

"Not unusual. Could I be of help? Are you hungry?"

"I guess … I guess I am."

He put his hand on my shoulder and led me around the corner. "Then you must eat. My name is Simon. Let me show you a wonderful place to be nourished."

Nourished? I found his choice of words odd, yet I immediately felt a comfort in his touch, not unlike my father's hand when he was still alive.

It was only a short distance until I saw the sign that hung above the sidewalk showing the entrance to Teachers Café. The day was bright with a natural light that electrified all the colors in my sight. Yet it was such a gentle light—like gossamer lace—that I ruminated over the idea that I could see so well, yet I needed no sunglass to sooth my eyes. Simon led me inside and guided me to a stool at the counter just as a man burst through the saloon doors that led to the kitchen.

"Teach," Simon said. "I have a customer for you. He's hungry, and I knew you would be just the ticket to conquer his appetite. Though he is a little confused at the surroundings."

"So it would seem," Teach replied.

Simon left with a pat to my back, and I sat wondering how he knew of my confusion, my chin resting on the web of my hand.

"So what would you like?" Teach asked.

The question caught my attention. As though but a moment had passed, I wanted to thank Simon, yet as I turned, I realized he was already gone from sight. Teachers Café was full of customers. I never noticed customers on the way in, and now I could feel apprehension pulling taut the ropes of my stomach. Nothing seemed as it should be. The air was too fresh, the day too clear, and all the people in the café looked too familiar. The only person who appeared to be a stranger was Teach.

My mind reeled: Was I drugged? The euphoria I was feeling could only be induced by some sort of drug, I surmised. Paranoia was a side effect of some powerful hallucinogens, I knew. That had to be what was happening. If I went along, the euphoria was ever present. Only when I questioned my situation came the hint of paranoia.

"So, son, are you hungry, or are you just going to sit there with your mouth open like a baby bird waiting for his mother?" Teach asked.

"Sorry, I'm just trying to get my bearings."

"Not unusual," he replied. "I have a chicken-fried steak special today. You want that?"

I nodded my head and started searching my arms for needle marks. Curiously, I didn't find any, not a blemish, and the scar on my forearm from the car wreck in 1984 was gone. Vanished without a trace.

The paranoia was back. I took a deep breath and gathered my thoughts. What I was sensing had to be a dream. It wasn't real. I was dreaming. I took another deep breath and released a fist of tension. Okay, sit back and go along, I told myself. There was nothing to fear. In fact, as dreams go, what I was encountering was not a nightmare, but the most pleasant illusion I had ever had.

Teach set a plate of food in front of me. Chicken fried steak, a baked sweet potato, corn on the cob—it was one of my favorite meals.

"Something to drink?"

"Yes. Water please."

Teach left, returning with a pitcher in his hand. "Sounds like you've had a pretty good life, wouldn't you say, friend?" He filled a glass in front of me with water and moved a napkin within my reach.

I had a mouth full of sweet potato, the taste was superb. "A good life? … Yes," I said after clearing my throat. "Of course, I have made a lot of good choices."

"How so?"

"Well, my father wanted me to take over the café. Come to think of it, it looked a lot like yours."

"Really?" he said with a quizzical air.

"Yeah," I said, pausing, my sight arcing over my shoulder. "But I went to college instead and got my degree. I've spent the last twenty-five years in medicine. I'm a doctor."

"How interesting."

"I know," I said, raising a palm like a stop sign. "First thing people think is: 'He went into it for the money.' But really, I just wanted to help people. The money was a gift."

"You've been very fortunate. Most people don't have the drive, or the opportunities for that matter, to pursue medicine."

"It's a tough road all right, but I overcame it."

"By the way, how is Madeleine?" he asked.

"My wife?" I stared at him, tried to see a wrinkle in his face that would let the dream come through. "She's fine," I said.

"Wonderful family. A boy, a girl ... the American dream."

"Well, it isn't easy, but I have always been a faithful and dedicated father."

"Never any thoughts of roaming," Teach grinned. "I mean, there are plenty of opportunities to stray."

"Well," I chuckled. "I'm no different from anyone else, but my philosophy has always been: Once you're married you can look ... okay, maybe let your mind wander on the dark side a bit ... but don't touch. It just costs too much in the long run."

"Yes, money is important."

"It's not just the money," I said adamantly. "I mean, I wouldn't want to hurt Madeleine ... or the kids." I took a bite of chicken fried steak. "Of course, I like money, don't get me wrong, but I don't believe all that crap, that 'money is the root of all evil.'"

Teach winked. "I think it's actually stated, 'For the love of money is a root of all kinds of evil.'"

"Whatever. I see nothing wrong with having it."

"I don't either," Teach said. "Besides, you look like a generous guy."

"I give my fair share. I mean taxes ... well, no one gets a kick out of paying taxes. However, I give money to United Way every year." A chuckle erupted from my chest. "Besides, it is easier to get them off the phone when you just shell out a few bucks and get it over with."

Teach moved off down the counter and rang up a donut and coffee. He was a tall man, stately, with friendly eyes. His hair was in a ponytail. I tore my way through the corn on the cob and was just wiping the butter from my chin when he returned.

"Sounds like you played by all the rules. Any regrets?"

"You mean about the past?"

"It has occurred to me that one can't get to the future without examining the past."

"I suppose you have a point." Memories flickered through my mind for a moment. Then I answered, "No, I don't have any regrets. I'm a good man by all standards, I think." Justification took a stroll through my conscience. "I mean, I don't cheat or steal, and I never murdered nobody, or committed adultery. Also, I helped my parents, may God bless them, until the day they died. My kids have successful careers, and they nor Madeleine have never lacked for anything."

"Strange choice of words," he replied.

"In what way?"

"Oh, I just mean you don't seem like the 'prayerful' type. 'May God bless them' I think you said."

I thought about the remark, trying to justify my statement. However, I always felt prayers were a crutch. "True," I said at length. "I was always told God helps those who help themselves. You must count on yourself first. I don't think God gets involved in the everyday situations of people's lives."

Teach seemed puzzled. "What does He get involved in?"

"Well, I guess, when you die you must fill him in on your life, and he determines your acceptability for heaven. But if you're a good person, no worries, right?"

"Sort of Buddhist mentality, wouldn't you think?"

"Call it what you want. I just feel you can find God anywhere. Like walk out in a forest. Or look at the ocean. If God isn't a part of all that … I mean somebody had to set off the firecracker that put the universe into motion."

"Good point."

"I just don't think you have to be crawling to God every five minutes with your every need. It's ludicrous to think he would have the time, or the capacity, to deal with all of us at that level. I am sure he has plenty of genuine problems to worry about besides people like me."

Teach smiled and began wiping down the counter.

"Just between you and me," I said. "Churches are a racket. It's just a business like owning a hardware store. You advertise, and people come in and buy what they want. I'm just not buying a lot of what they're selling. Heck, look at the Catholic Church, for instance. That's where I was raised. They have more rituals than a juju woman … it's mostly man-made stuff, by the way. No, if I need to pray, all I need to do is walk out into a forest and think about it."

"You spend a lot of time in the forest? I thought you were a doctor."

"You know what I mean. If I need God, I know where I can find Him."

"Would you like any dessert … maybe some coffee to wash that down?"

"No. Actually, I feel pretty good. I don't know if it was the food, or the conversation …" I gazed out the café window. "Or the surroundings, but I feel pretty content at the moment."

"Nourishment is my specialty."

I got up from my stool as if I had somewhere to go. "So, what do I owe you?"

"Everything," he replied.

I hesitated. "No really. How much was it?"

"Forget it. It was on the house. Besides, there's no way you can pay me for it, anyway."

I searched my pocket. "You're right. I'm broke. I don't even have a credit card." What a dream, I thought, but how was it going to end? I didn't feel threatened and there certainly wasn't anything erotic about Teach or the food. This was the craziest dream I'd ever experienced.

"So, are you ready?"

Suddenly, Simon was standing in front of me.

"Simon? Where did you come from?"

"I've got the car."

I looked around and Teach was gone. Teach, and all the people, had evaporated into thin air. Suddenly, I was sitting in the back of a 1955 Cadillac, black with button-tuck leather seats.

I succumbed to the moment. "Okay, so where are we headed?"

"Edge of town. From there, you'll be on your own."

I gazed out my window. Look at all these spectacular trees, I thought to myself. The bungalows were gone; just trees remained. A smile found its way to my mouth, and I giggled silently, for in my mind I could hear Teach's voice: 'Everything'. What did he mean by that? And for a moment, a brief jostling of my spirit, my heart filled with hope. Hope for my family.

But my smile eroded, and a lonely sigh left my lips. Like a guilty slap in the face; as Simon drove away from downtown, I realized his car had no handles on the inside. A piece of Plexiglas separated him and me, and I was trapped in the backseat. It was hot, steamy, as if I was somewhere in South Carolina or Georgia in mid-summer. A chill ran down my spine. I twisted in my seat, all at once uncomfortable. The air was getting hard to breathe. A thought provoked me: Trees … a forest. I'm in a forest. But that would mean …

I turned, putting a knee up on the cushion, and with the palm of my hand, wiped a hole in the accumulating breath on the rear window. A small hole, but through it, all things became clear. The bright light that was once Teacher's Café was fading fast in the expanding distance. Above me, ominous clouds were poised in the sky, swirling down behind the car like smoke from an oil fire. A flock of birds raced inland, seeking shelter. The trees, once green with foliage, were now scorched, standing like silent sentinels of disaster along the road. I slipped down in my seat, my muscles suddenly heavy, my heart now just an echo unto itself.

In the front seat, Simon had disappeared, replaced by a man with a nose that looked phallic and obscene. I remembered church as a child being this quiet—except the man in the front seat was gnashing his teeth, and the sound was growing louder and louder and louder.

Minutes later, the car turned onto a gravel road. Rocks cracked against the floorboards. I sat up straight and gripped the edge of the seat with my hands.

"Who was that man?" I cried. "Teach, who was he?"

The man in the front seat snickered. I could smell his foul breath, his body rife with the stench of dead animals. "Jesus, my friend. That was Jesus." Then he laughed. A roiling laugh that erupted boils across my back. "Didn't you know him?" he said. "John Michael McGee … a man of the forest indeed!"

I tried to hold back, but the boils were searing with pain, and I felt an alkaline tear burn the flesh down my cheek, my eyes red with the blood of my children, my grandchildren, and theirs ad infinitum.

I suffer now in a forsaken world; the same one I was deceived into believing was not real. I recognize no one. No one recognizes me. It is vacant and cold of emotion, except the anguish that smolders rancid in the hollow of my chest. I will never feel the love of Jesus Christ, only the torment of my abusers, here where my name is uttered in whispers as one would a lewd remark.

Forever yours,
John Michael McGee

***

I still have the letter. It never leaves my pocket. I cannot explain it, nor will I ever try, for I have learned not to waste my life being too proud or intelligent to accept God's ways. My fate may be sealed.

Only God knows if I wrote that letter and threw it into the River Styx—it was my signature after all—but if I can save one soul by knowing of the letter's existence, I will have fulfilled the purpose that was intended.

For me, discovering the letter has refocused my commitments. The Bible has become my obedience, for my opinion of His Scriptures is of no interest to God.

God the Father, Jesus and the Holy Spirit are One; a mystery sure, however, the path for me is simpler than I imagined. No one lives their life well enough to gain admission to heaven. Jesus died for my sins. He paid the price for admission. It's a gift. His gift to give. My job is to accept the gift by believing in Him.

Or let me put it another way. I see now that the accurate measure of a man finds value in the only commodity that Jesus cannot or will not command: Love. He wants a loving relationship with us. But He won't force us.

When I fell in love with Madeleine, I wanted to learn everything about her. I adored her. I wanted to spend my life in her presence. God wants no more from us, or no less.

That is why I will spend the rest of my earthly life reaching and seeking for God's hand, so that I will know Him, Jesus, when my day comes. For Heaven is granted by His grace alone, not by the foolish tally of my good works.

So, take heed of the deception that the world would like us to believe; don't wait for a bottle filled with Truth. We are not promised next year, next week, nor even our next breath. When death comes, you will be alone, as I, with no one to rely on, with no science to provide the answers, naked of your accomplishments, traveling a course into another existence, this time for eternity.

AGAINST ALL ODDS

Preface

A nd behold, a certain lawyer stood up and tested Him, saying, "Teacher, what shall I do to inherit eternal life?" (Luke 10:25 NKJV)

So he [Jesus] answered and said, " 'You shall love the Lord your God with all your heart, with all your soul, with all your strength, and with all your mind,' and 'your neighbor as yourself.' " (Luke 10:27 NKJV)

My parents came from humble beginnings and ended in humble legacy. For over sixty years they were together, and through it all they never lost sight of what was important.

Against All Odds

Stare at the horizon and imagine sixty years
How the porcelain blue of heaven, finds the rooted brown of earth
How together they are married
From their union the world was birth.

Such as it was, for both man and wife
She of porcelain, fragile, yet constant still
He of rooted earth, simple, solid, provider
Their marriage a mingling of wills.

So take a moment to wonder
Let your thoughts be focused with mine
See the depth of this day before us
Their accomplishment beyond our time.

Bitter cold; hail from a Midwestern sky
Land that spewed rocks in the spring
Money scarce as dust in the wind
No count for a diamond ring.

Labor endless as the ocean tide
From morning till night, hard times
Through sickness, and wars, and presidents
Yet against all odds they survived.

And we wonder at the ability, the commitment, the strength
To weather six children in stride
Today we see two as a heroic feat
Now wonder how many nights they cried.

God laid plans for their life in the beginning
As a smith, hammered them into gold
Look around you; take a good look at you and me
In your sight their purpose unfolds.

For my father is like a whetstone,
His children sharpened against the grain.
And my mother pliant as the willow tree,
Providing shelter from the rain.

So lest not forget it is because of them
Their faith in the Lord above
No matter what life has prepared for us
We can handle it; we have their love.

ARI NUI AND THE GREEN FLASH

Preface

The green flash is an optical phenomenon that sometimes occurs transiently around the moment of sunrise or sunset. When the conditions are right, a distinct green flash is briefly visible above the Sun's upper limb; the green appearance usually lasting for less than two seconds. Typically seen on an unobstructed horizon, such as over the ocean, it may occur at any latitude, although at the equator, the flash rarely lasts longer than a second.

Ari Nui was a Filipino boy, age six or seven, whom I met on a catamaran called the Na Hoku II in Waikiki. He and his father were traveling to Malaysia, where his father was starting a charter boat business.

When the Green Flash appeared at sunset, rising up over the ocean, I could not help but think God had fashioned a sign for Ari Nui, and that day, Ari Nui and the Green Flash had risen to superhero status.

ARI NUI AND THE GREEN FLASH

Beyond the horizon, where stories live to be told,
Ari Nui set sail for the curve of the earth,
A pencil-line mystery drawn across his future,
Chapter of life to be written today.

Out from the shore, voices rise and mingle,
Confused, sharp as the cackle of sea birds
Plundering the remnants of dinner, fading
In the wake of ripples in silver words.

Will he come today is the wonder, gazing
At our feet peppered by Abraham's descendants,
Feeling the sun flare and tattoo the skin, women
With the scent of hibiscus lingering in their hair.

The sails of Na Hoku flap yellow-red, billowing
Triangles of wind, as creation divides beneath her hull.
Lazy roll of sea turtle, dolphin dance at her bow,
Invisible reins pulling our carriage through water.

Do you know his whereabouts, Diamond Head,
Or hear the salt sea whispers from watery graves
Singing the lure of the siren songs, barren witness
To ships laden with cargo disappearing in his light.

From where does the wind blow, Ari Nui,
As does our hearts from some unseen force
To carry this vessel across the waves, and rolls,
Whitecaps glistening in the vanishing sun.

Soon the moon will rise gray to blue craters
As echoes of the falling night settle over Waikiki,
Where Tiki torches flicker the stars in a paradise sky,
And dark-skinned beauties sheen the eyes of men.

While Ari Nui stands akimbo at the helm, raven hair,
Shy smile, his old friend Green Flash appears.
Our hearts soar, sun making its escape from the day,
Glint of ray through a crest at the edge of the earth.

Imagine what adventures Ari Nui and the Green Flash await,
Sailing for Indonesian waters, even now, where pirates
Bound in the evening heat, and legends are borne
At midnight from the twist of liars and truth.

BETWEEN
THE MOON AND ME

Preface

For many years, the Love-Joy-Peace (LJP) house in Depot Bay, Oregon, was a refuge. At the time, my wife and I were leading a ministry called Alpha at our church, and LJP would graciously allow us to retreat to the house free-of-charge. The Alpha years from 2002 to 2011 were a special season in our life, and a time of enormous spiritual growth for us personally.

The LJP house overlooked Pirates Cove to the west and was rimmed by trees on the south. I had many opportunities to gaze out the living room window across the ocean and contemplate what God had in-store for us next.

BETWEEN THE MOON AND ME

Between the moon and me
Sets a silver horizon
Trees dressed in shimmer
Water mercurial in the cast
Reach for the ridge
Arms stretched to the promise
No looking back, taking stock
Bright lies the road ribbon
Focus the wind
Heart and soul tendered
Payment due

CAUGHT IN THE RIPPLE

Preface

This picture rests in a nice wooden frame on my office credenza. I was seventeen. It is a gentle reminder to me that the faith I had in God at that age was my parents. I was safe in the womb of my upbringing. Then I left home, and my faith was left behind. After many transgressions, God helped me rise from the ashes, and life since then became a journey, finding my way back to that mountain stream.

CAUGHT IN THE RIPPLE

Crouched in the middle of a stream
Unbeknown of the future
Caught in the ripple
Cool waters tickle my toes
Smile face at the wonder
Risen from the ashes
Spirit soar above the mountains
Spy down the valleys
For love has come from vapor
Breath of God
And it takes me to the ends of the earth.

CENTER OF MY DESIRE

Preface

From 2002 to 2011, my wife and I led a ministry at our church called Alpha. We had two eleven-week sessions a year, and about week six we would have a retreat. At our first retreat, we had sixteen people. At our last, we had over one-hundred-sixty.

We called the retreat our Holy Spirit Weekend, and each Saturday night was an overwhelming engagement of the Holy Spirit through prayer. So each Saturday morning, I would wake up early and find a place to sit and wait for the Lord to speak. I was sitting on this log when he gave me these words.

CENTER OF MY DESIRE

The trees in leaf as the days grow long to summer.
The ever-changing canvas He paints over my head.
The flit of sparrow as it darts from limb to tree.
The call of the Meadowlark in search of food.

In that place where time and space cease to exist,
Where love is the only dimension, and joy
The measure of our days.

He calls to me in the morning,
Bright shower of gifts for the day.
He waits at the edge of the meadow,
The tree line the perimeter of His court,
And there in this quiet place, He charts
The compass of my day.

CRADLE
AGAINST THE DOOR

Preface

Politics aside, my experience with abortion is my own. As a young man, the ability to abort my child was too easy and too acceptable; even in the 1970s. At first, I tried to vindicate myself, stating that the mother did not give me a choice, but truthfully, I would've most likely come to the same conclusion on my own.

Years later, the shame I feel is real, but I can only imagine how a mother resolves the pain she carries in her empty womb. This poem is my attempt to encapsulate that pain, even though I know I fall woefully short in that endeavor.

CRADLE AGAINST THE DOOR

Trapped in a chamber of my own design,
The winter snow, the fetus lies steaming.
My fetus in a barrel by the barn.

Dreadful winter.
The logs of my cabin sweat with foul humidity,
Burning flesh of my soul, branded
While the blood of new life escapes the steel confines
Into breathless vapor.

Here is my cradle against the door,
Once made for a baby's coos, now
Stopping the Lord from coming in.
Freedom so sought after, lost
To another lie.

Truth be it: The choice before passion,
Not after the miracle has begun.
I am such a fool: My burden
Is lessened by this act?
What course of mankind will I travel
For self-indulgence?
Can I rationalize my baby is now in a better place?
Did I prepare the hummingbird in its struggle to fly?
Did I form the ocean to be the hub in the spokes of life?
What then prepared me for this decision?
My knowledge of the future?

My heart is torn with incompletion.
My chest filled with liquid rage.
I weep until my eyes are red …
Red with the blood of my unborn children.

Dare I say: "To be human
Is to be made in the image of God,"
For love be at our center, if not,
Only evil remains, and love has left me today.

I have let the voices toll
My future: "Humanity over God,"
As I ventured headlong from the truth,
Deceived into thinking,
I should have no part in God, as if
I was my own creation.

With each lick of my ears, the sorghum sound, the lies
Flowed like water from his mouth,
Slowly the weight countered,
Wheels turned reason against reason,
My soul like grist in the devil's mill.

Oh, but my disgust is in vain.
All that is left now is the empty shell,
Hollow with sorrow and shame,
Freedom of choice chained by guilt.

I cannot deny it,
A piece of me has left today never to return,
A piece of my soul sent without me to wait.
Shall I stack another cradle by the door?
The fruit of another lover to block the entrance.
Shall I grease the porch with hurry, or opiates,
To keep the Truth at bay?
Or replace the locks with keys from some other
More calculating god, the tally of eternal atonement
Grinding false notches on its shank.

No, I am trapped inside this cabin of guilt
By my own design, until
I can push aside my imperfection
With hands of grace.
In my mind's eye I see,
Each day I wait, bitterness will salt my wound, until
I am but a festering sore of the woman
That was once Eve.

I must fling the door wide open, infernal heat escape,
Before there is time for confusion to rear his ugly head.
Before it's too late, let the forgiveness of Spring replace
The temporal lust that wintered my heart.
Be quick!
Let Him, who first charted the universe, replenish my soul
With His warm caress, the sweet taste of my eternal lover
On my lips as I bid him a bow to come in.

EVERYTHING IS NEW

PREFACE

When our season in Portland, Oregon, was over, God made it clear we needed to move. "Go to the desert and learn from a brilliant teacher," was what we heard. Then He put into place all the pieces that were needed for us to go, including the pastor whom God positioned squarely in our path, the very first Sunday we arrived in Tucson, Arizona.

Even though God didn't mention how hard the first six months would be; in the end, He was right, and now thirteen-years later, we are right where we are supposed to be.

EVERYTHING IS NEW

Everything is new
The horizon is straight
Mountaintops etched clear
Against a Tombstone sky

No one can tell me
What is, or what will be,
It's mine, me alone
Yet not alone

The finch with its golden feather
Drinks at the well, the roadrunner
Stalks a rattlesnake at dawn
I too am my own destiny

I will look to the border
I will gaze at the desert sky
And wonder upon great wonder
In my grasp I see

The beauty that lies before
Me in a desert willow, oleander
Strong and silent saguaro
I am

FINGERPRINTS

PREFACE

Jesus said, mother, I couldn't stay another day longer
He flies right by and leaves a kiss upon her face
While the angels were singing his praises in a blaze of glory
Mary stays behind and starts cleaning up the place
(Mary, Patti Griffin, Flaming Red, Track 12)

The Virgin Mary is the epitome of strength; of courage; of obedience. She watched as her firstborn son blossomed into a man of God. Then watched him be crucified for the sins of mankind. Yet she knew it had to be so and never ceased to support Him.

My mother left her mark on everything she touched, especially me, her imperfect son. She never gave up on me. She had all the attributes of Mary. Her death left a hole in the earth. Her resurrected life awaits me in heaven.

FINGERPRINTS

With trepidation I kneel at the edge of the crevasse, knowing,
No matter my mental strength I cannot cast my thoughts
To the other side—I see my words arcing downward, plummeting
Like a cold stone, only to ring hollow on the path where she stood.

Covered in roses, covered in ashes, covered in pain, her fingerprints
Are everywhere, the room is empty, the bed without sheets, yet
I feel them in my hair, on my cheek, caressing my wounds
Where my plans melted into tragedy, and tragedy into guilt.

In my mind's eye I stood at the window, weight on
my hands, gazing
At the willow tree, draping its reflection in a pond,
and there she was
Swinging on my father's arm in a field, sweet grin of
invincible youth,
Destiny and hope and love and children bright upon her face.

"Baby Boy—My baby boy"—how simple she was,
how her words tore
At my heart, as I held her close and felt the hair on her neck bristle
Against my fingers, to kiss her cheek and she kiss mine,
one last time,
How graceful she was in her simplicity, like sunshine and gold.

FINGERPRINTS

I have no doubt where she walks this day, that young man
With his head tilted onto hers, smitten, heart aching with poetry
For her, holding close, more in love now than ever
before, endless …
Thoughts of days past, struggle, lost in dreams and spatters of light.

I lament the games I played to manipulate her affection, thinking
I had to coerce a love that she gave so freely, so boldly, so clear
My mind now dear Lord of any regret, for she
never wanted penance
Only hugs and smiles and a child's face in
her apron and to comb my hair.

Uncommon she was, though she came from common birth,
Steadfast she stood, in a world that wavers and caves, a spirit
Given from God and taken to His side, where she belongs, a sign
Of things to come and a signpost to follow on a crooked path.

Our Father in heaven, hallowed be thy name, thy kingdom come
Thy will be done, I praise your Holy name for a mother such as this
For me, undeserving, unworthy of the best, yet given
a Mary, a mother
Of virgin character, of Heaven, and she
goes about cleaning up the place.

Look over my shoulder she is there, look into the forest she is there
Look into the future she is there, look at my brothers and
sister she is there
Look to the grandchildren she is there, look at a willow tree
or a glass ball
On the ocean, or a plain music box playing Oklahoma,
and she is there.
Her fingerprints are everywhere.

FOR THE LOVE
OF A DAUGHTER

PREFACE

My daughter and I have a special bond: from the day she was born, I was her primary caregiver. Not that her mother didn't love her, but circumstances of health stood in the way.

Then as she grew older, the world began to tug us apart. It is how God intended it to be. She had to become independent to fulfill the role of mother she was destined to be. Yet that season of life was hard.

There had been words between us. Words that cut deep and healed thin, and she decided she had to move on.

Yet the Holy Spirit had a plan, and she ended up in Scotland in a Youth With A Mission (YWAM) clan, deep in discipleship training, and it changed her life, and mine. She spent six months in Scotland and three months in South Africa and Mozambique. The day I left her in Scotland, I knew we had crossed a bridge. The poem reflects what it meant to say goodbye.

FOR THE LOVE OF A DAUGHTER

My love for you, daughter, is without question,
Deep as the ocean and wide as the sky,
Emerging at birth, a seedling rooted in my soul,
Intricate yet strong, to flower for eternity.

I remember the first step, the first cry,
The first utterance of my name,
The way you curled upon my chest,
Your breath light upon my neck.

When the quiet of morning gave promise,
When the solace of evening echoed the day,
I found wonder in your perfection,
The smell of innocence in your hair.

God had given me a gift in the midst of despair,
A treasure to be protected beyond my own life.
I took to the duty with fervor it seemed,
Poured out my love in endless streams of emotion.

Yet as a bolt of lightning splits the sky,
There was a crack in the plate of my existence.
Brought there by the first fallen heroes,
The fist of God angry upon their hearts.

No matter how carefully I washed it,
Or placed it on the shelf, the crack grew,
Splintering into veins of failure and disappointment,
Unaffected by the glue of my prideful will.

I could not change it, I cannot still
It is beyond my power to heal the shards.
But if my love cannot mend it, so great as it is for you,
Who then or what then can be the salve?

In this world, no greater love exists or endures,
This father to his child, yet I have failed you.
So true to my mind, a tear at my heart, how can it be?
Not out of malice, nor rejection, but love?

See true love is imperfect in this place, impossible to attain.
Though sonnets profess it, and our lips so easily proclaim it,
Love is strangled by mortal ambition, left untarnished
Only in the minds of poets and fools and
schoolgirls with trusting smiles.

Therefore I give you back to God from whence you came,
Not discarded—oh child hear my heart as it bleeds the page,
But alive in the hope that only His love can secure.
For I am limited in my virtue, He is limitless in His grace.

Make no doubt, I will always be your father, here
To love you with the full extent of my heart,
But compared to me, His house is filled with ageless wonders.
The universe is His footstool, and He has called you to His throne.

So place your love for Him above all others,
Just as He loved you first before you were mine.
The agony He endured was so that you would not have to
For the love of a daughter—He gave His life.

FOR THE LOVE OF A SON

PREFACE

As fortunate as I was to raise my daughter, I did not get the same chance with my son. Divorce has an ugly way of ripping apart what God has glued together.

I am a fixer by nature, and although I was allowed to see him every other weekend, I couldn't repair the damage, and it left me in despair. I wanted him to know how much I loved him, and as usual my remedy was to write, so that someday, he may read my words and know the truth.

FOR THE LOVE OF A SON

Hollow is my heart
I shout but the echoes desert me
Like a rock falling into a deep well
The splash is so quiet
It may have been tears

You are the arm
That has been severed
The leg that atrophied
In the dark
While you were taken away

You are part of me
Yet not part of me
You are here
Yet you are not here
A myth born of me

Like a ghost
I feel you
Shiver on my spine
Your breath
Whispery like rain

I wish I could hug you
I wish I could hold you
I wish I could smell
Then rustle your hair
Now, not later

I pray to the Lord
Everyday
That you are the better parts of me
That you will grow and know
I am with you

As I cannot at times
God has put His arms
Around you
For me
And watched over you

I pray he has told you
The good things about me
That you will feel it in your chest
Like a gasp
When you see me

All those nights
When you went to bed alone
And I wasn't there
Understand
I was thinking of you

Your name
Branded on my heart
I will take to my grave
For you are mine
No other's

Imagine
Hollow as a well
Imagine that in your chest
The nothingness
The void

Cold and darkness
Surround you
A rock may fall
To the bottom
I have been

Love
Sucked away
Like so much blood
Sucked from my heart
Never from my soul

For the way you roll your eyes
The way you giggle and laugh
The way your ticklish on the ribs
The way you fight me at bedtime
I love all those things

The way you're so scared
To try new things
Yet once bitten, no looking back
Taking it with all the fury
That God has put within you

I am proud of the way
You love to read
I am proud of the way
You love to be precise
That's you

I am proud of the way
You take such joy in little things
Orange kitties
Patrick and Spongebob
Playing basketball

Praising God as you do
Perfect childish way
Riding your bike
The nature park where we run
And see beavers and birds

FREEDOM

PREFACE

My good friend got married to a wonderful gal. Their wedding was held at Roche Harbor in the San Juan Islands. A fitting place, for they both love the water and cruising on their boat.

We all went there for the weekend to celebrate, and once I got there, God downloaded a message to me for them. The world has told us that marriage is the end of freedom, that the wedding ring is really a ball and chain. However, God wanted them to know that they had made the right decision, and they had embarked on the ultimate freedom.

I can say with exuberance that He was right, and it seems to me they are more in love today than the day they got married so many years ago. Amazing how well things work out when we follow the Creator's plan.

FREEDOM

Ancient is the story they live
Timeless is the truth they portray
For back in the Garden it was, even then
The same story as today.

He comes forth a son of Adam
Created in the wilderness, a fierce
And brandished heart, as all men
Wild at the core of his being.

She comes forth a daughter of Eve
Created in the image, lush Eden
The crown jewel of His creation
Most intricate flower saved for last.

A man, he has waited for a battle to fight,
Soul longing for an adventure to live.
He has searched his realm through forest and glen,
His eye kept wide for a beauty to rescue.

A woman, she has waited patiently, yearning
To be fought for, longing for an adventure to share.
Within the tower she has concealed
Her riches, her beauty to unveil.

FREEDOM

Let not the battle ever be won,
For in the conquest lies the secret of love.

Let not the adventure ever to end,
For in the journey is life, with so much to share.

Let not the rescue ever be thwarted,
For it is in the struggle that beauty reveals.

You were created in the image of God,
Male and female, the traits of His personality
Beyond our imagination, so now you can be one
As He intended, symbols of His majesty.

So take diligence that the roles you were created to live
Are not twisted, forgotten, or left unattended.
For man must fight the battle; woman must be the prize.
Man must lead the adventure; woman must be by his side.
Man must sacrifice for beauty, which woman kindles deep inside.

In this lies the ultimate freedom
Against the teachings of the world
Against the wandering of the flesh, a future
Bright with love, ripe with commitment, as one
Found in the Garden, walking in the cool of the day.

GOD'S GRACE

PREFACE

This is a simple poem based on Ephesians 4: 26-27 (NKJV): "Be angry, and do not sin": do not let the sun go down on your wrath, nor give place to the devil; and Nehemiah 8:10 (NJKV): "… Do not sorrow, for the joy of the Lord is your strength."

What would we do without the encapsulating words of God?

GOD'S GRACE

Never let the sun set on an argument,
Never let the sun rise without an embrace.
Always remember the joy you feel tonight,
For in its strength lies the power of grace.

I CAN REMEMBER

PREFACE

I had an idyllic childhood. My parents were home every night and allowed me to roam the rural countryside at will. My Aunt Mary and Uncle George lived two houses away. I could have hot dogs and corn any time I wanted. Next to them, lived my grandparents. I could walk to school, which was directly behind my house, and I had access to five baseball diamonds, all within a five-minute-walking distance; and baseball was my favorite sport.

In addition, with my .22 rifle or fishing pole propped onto the handlebars of my bicycle, I could reach a great hunting or fishing spot in less than thirty minutes. Besides that, I was the fastest runner and smartest kid in my class. What could go wrong?

I started drinking at fourteen. I started smoking pot at eighteen. From there, I ventured from the idyllic countryside of youth into the pit of hell until I was thirty-two.

I CAN REMEMBER

I can remember as a child growing up in a big old house
in the country,
With a narrow front porch, and stairs that creaked every
time you tried to sneak,
And my Aunt Mary and Uncle George bless their hearts,
Who had none but took me for their very own.

I can remember the smell of cookies in the kitchen while I
took a nap, boiling coffee,
The sound of the sprinkler outside my summer window,
whirling out its rainbows across the lawn;
The click of the oscillating fan blowing its coolness
across my face, a twist of fresh cut grass on the wind.

As a child in this place I remember too untying Dad's
leather boots when he got home from work, the enormous
hug, the barrel chest, stretching my arms to barely touch my
fingertips at his back, the smell of sawdust on his clothes,
the blue in his eyes.

Or sitting at mom's feet while she embroidered pillowcases,
Her taking a moment to run a finger through my hair.
The sound of her jewelry box playing Oklahoma.
The warm, safe feel of her apron against my cheek.

Life has always been mottled like the sun through the trees,
Shifting patterns of light and dark against the ground.
The footpath we must walk, the soil slick beneath our feet.
Not always two steps forward, but one-step back.

Yet even though I have wandered in the dark, and the dark
has wandered over me,
My parents always encouraged me to live in the light.
The glass half full, not half empty.
No matter the storm they were always there to tie
up to, anchors.

So I guess what I want to say to them now is that: "Home
was a great place to grow up."
Should all children be so lucky.
Those times I said, "I want to blow this hole,"
were just the ramblings of idle youth.

I HAVE
PONDERED THE TREES

PREFACE

As with the poem *Center of My Desire*, this poem was born at an Alpha retreat in Rockaway Beach, when I would get up early Saturday morning to find a place to visit and wait for the Lord to speak.

I walked a path meandering through the woods, crossing a small creek, my surroundings covered in rainforest moss. It is hard to ignore God when nature cries out His name.

I HAVE PONDERED THE TREES

I have pondered the trees
The generations in their grasp
Rooted in our existence, strong and silent
Angels in our midst

I have followed the streams of cool water,
Bubbling mirth on their lips
Winding from the fountainheads of men
Springing up from wells on the family land

I have heard the ocean roar,
Turbulent skin fighting among the rocks
Harboring life beyond the mirage,
As truth abounds in soaring depths

I have felt the rain light upon my face
Turn on me into a pelting sting
How quickly it soaked my clothes, growing heavy
Even as flowers burst along my path

I have seen the sun flickering
Lost in the distance
Deceived by clouds in the valley
Bright as neon at the mountaintop I climb

Such is creation around us,
From the ground where we bury our dead,
To the heavens
Where death has no voice

Friends set as guideposts
For our journey beyond understanding
1st century to 1st century
As if 2000 years never passed.

IN HER EYES

PREFACE

This photo is from the Oregon Coast, more importantly from the backyard of a special woman whom I instantly felt a connection to. She was the mother of a friend. She had amyotrophic lateral sclerosis, commonly known as ALS.

The first time we met, she could not speak but still could move freely around her house and property. The second time we met, she could not move, I was told, except for her foot to signal yes or no. Yet, to everyone's surprise, she smiled at me, and her eyes spoke volumes to my soul.

What she conveyed to me was peace and love, powerful and bold. She died shortly after that second visit.

IN HER EYES

I did not know your mother
As one knows a friend of years
How she would gaze at the fire in a sunset
Or the threat of anger brought her eyes to tears.

She was but an acquaintance after all
A happen stance, a series of turns
In a road that led me here, my loss
Not knowing her before, I learned.

Yet I remember the first time I met her
From the corner of my eye, as if it were etched in glass
Forever in my vision, caught on the canvas of my mind
No solvent could erase her, no alcohol in my grasp.

So there she was, a milestone in my life
Though a jaded memory it must be, a sour wine
For the fear in her eyes stayed with me for days
Like a sickness, viral, unable to cure, only time.

The pain of lost conversation
She sat at the edge wanting in
Not knowing then how to play this game
Her deck cut short, her hand left thin.

Then as the days stretched between us
Facts and reason found it hard to adhere
The torment she endured was reduced to rumor
Again my life, my surroundings, had no fear.

'Til the hands of time came marching
As a clock returns to the beginning of each day
Where soon I found myself confronting the unknown
Having to visit this woman of clay.

So I thought I would find this person
Weak and fragile, conquered, ready to shatter into dust
Like a jar filled with anguish and sorrow
Thrust upon the rocks of God's mistrust.

But alas, my lessons are far from complete
With each breath of life I must learn
For in her eyes the last time we touched
I found peace and love, not spurn.

She smiled and her eyes beat deep in my chest
God was there in this body wracked with ill
Pain and suffering may be eased by drugs
But salvation is free, not a pill.

She had been transformed, reborn of thought
As though a rainbow had crested the tear-soaked sky
For surrounded by death her heart held fast
Her body would succumb, her love would not die.

Her children's touch, their voices such joy
She held it in the folds of her soul
Welling there like a fountain of truth
Heaven's eternity looming gold.

From her I will carry this essence
For I have seen it now firsthand
There is no fear in ending this life
We're going back to where we began.

Born in love, we'll die the same
Leaving love in our wake His command
So be proud and joyous she was yours
For no finer woman has blessed this land.

Remember always what she taught me
Though our encounters were quiet and brief
Love all your life, your family, your friends, smile for heaven awaits
Stand strong and pure, be happy as well, spirit conquering grief.

IN THE DESERT OF MY MALCONTENT

PREFACE

My brother tells me I am melancholy. My wife tells me I am moody. God tells me I have the gift of exhortation and craftsmanship. I guess I am all those things. I don't think it is a complete list.

However, because of how He made me, sometimes God takes me places in my mind. Low places conjured out of my past. Lonely places. *In the Desert of My Malcontent* is one of those places.

Life is a struggle, but I am reminded that even though I may be stuck in a cave like David, God is there.

IN THE DESERT OF MY MALCONTENT

In the desert of my malcontent
There lies a foot upon my chest
My breath hard against the unseen force
Of emptiness

Lord I cry out, Mercy!
For I am lost wandering where you are not
Lying without rest in the mud
Of your creation

Oh! Lord show me your greatness,
Tap my shoulder with the remembrance
Of your spirit

I walk unable to flourish
Because the water has been cut
To a trickle and my blooms have died
Without cause

Oppression be on me thick
As smoke from an oil fire—Oh to breathe
Clean air and sense your touch at the base
Of my mind.

Lift me Lord above the ashes,
Blast the stronghold with your mighty wind, I am
Prostrate with frustration eating at my bones
Sore anger and self-pity
Fill my bed

Mercy—Mercy! Give me strength to see distant
The end of day. Bless my tent and gird the animals
That drag me through thistle and brush, and let not
Your presence be away from me, left parched in the desert
Of my malcontent.

I am tired of the administration of life and wish
for the calm fullness of love and joy which exists
not beyond but within
my labor.

LIFE IN A BOX

PREFACE

I think a lot about the end of life. Not morbidly, but cast in the calculation of purpose and legacy. How well did I do with what God gave me? How well did I love those entrusted to my care?

Lots of unanswered questions, but one day, I will sail across the eternal horizon and leave those shores behind.

LIFE IN A BOX

What is it that made me worry?
Children, marriage, past indiscretions
My hand holds my brow
In anguish.

Can I be free?
Can I walk out of here?
It's all gone bad—my beauty
Where am I now?

In the womb
Of my Mother, my Father's joy
All bars broken, fresh sheet of paper
Smells all clean and new.

Give me another pen
Let Twain muse my Mississippi
Let Hemingway prose my plight
I want more of love but have so little.

For my children, the best, only
I try too hard, futile limits
How can I redo the moments?
Those already lost.

It isn't about me, my triumphs
My failures, the abhorrence I see
But my legacy, my daughter
My son, my prize, I see it now.

God reaches his hand
How do I grasp it? Let me walk,
Give me sail; my legs are weak
And time is running away.

My breath is slow; all is milk
Around me; bombs are bursting
Celebration and ending
I see the lights of paradise.

MARY'S SONG

PREFACE

My Aunt Mary was a special woman. She had four children. All of them died before they reached the age of nine days. It was due to Rh incompatibility. Modern medicine has cured this dilemma, but in her day, it was almost certain death.

When I was young, I spent almost every day at her house. I called her Mary Cramer. She fed me hot dogs and corn, and she made me feel as if I was the luckiest kid alive because I had two mothers. My mom didn't care. With six kids, she could use the help.

When she passed away, I wrote her this song. By then I had gone my way of unfortunate choices and had seen my share of struggle. Some I brought on myself. Some just came on their own.

I should've spent more time with her during those years. I could've learned many things from her, especially about faith. She was a giant of faith, in my eyes, Abraham giant. For no matter what life threw at her, she never let pity or bitterness poison her relationship with God.

MARY'S SONG

As the sun arose this morning,
I found myself on a mountaintop of Faith,
Gazing down at the wonder of the world,
Rivers and flowers and tumbling surf,
Left only to imagine the Garden and all its splendor.

For in some distant land beyond our recollection,
Treachery and lies have taken us from its view,
Peace and joy to be doled out as commodities,
To be bought and sold, traded for gold,
Left in a world where darkness shades our eyes.

In my younger years, caught in sorrow's grasp,
I entertained the lie, so cleverly disguised,
Thought mine was the only pain to be reconciled,
Convicted the Lord for the injustice in my life,
And searched for heaven where it does not exist.

Raising the hammer high over my head,
I splintered my life into sharp points of agony,
Each blow a remorseful reckoning,
Hope crushed by an iron fist,
Knowing my life was my will, not His.

Slivers of self-pity festered beneath my skin,
I searched for joy in the amber of alcohol,
Peace in the den of chemical addiction,
Pleasure with the charge of lustful eyes,
And abundant anguish followed my days.

I never imagined losing a child as Mary did,
Never thought to look around, to see
From the eyes of another more tested than I,
Her child taken mere hours into breath,
A hole the size of his life left in her heart.

Not once, but twice did she feel this knife,
Slice through her throat of happiness,
While countless others died within her womb,
Her loving arms never to caress,
Her soft voice never to whisper their names.

Hers was not an easy life, blessed with great wealth,
Immune from the curse of crippling disease,
More like a sail in a tempest, yet one constant held true,
Steady today, the same constant that split time in two,
Faith in her Savior, her anchor post of life.

Not as I, when caught in sorrow's grasp,
She found joy in the amber sunrise of creation,
Peace in the folded hands of prayer,
Pleasure in the hearts of children,
Not her own, if there was a difference.

Why shouldn't we place faith in the earth?
Surely the sun will rise and fall each day,
Summer will come after Spring, we've seen.
Yet for many, Eternity looms lonely as a ship,
Disappearing from the horizon on an endless wave.

For Mary, Eternity has come to take her home.
There her crown is filled with many jewels,
Her arms large enough to encompass all her children,
Her love as deep as the ocean still,
For the man she lost, and heaven restored.

Her test here now lies behind her,
The Promise ahead beyond our imagination.
As years melt into moments, true joy and love have come real,
Forever like a blanket to keep her warm,
Savoring the fruit of her life, God's purpose fulfilled.

Basking in the Light of His face,
Like a summer day, He has come to take her.
Almighty, powerful, shining beyond space and time,
Peaceful, loving, a father revered above the earth,
Her lungs have been filled with anticipation.

Throughout her life she set forth with eyes to see,
And ears to hear, she trusted Him as a child.
Why not her reward be so great that our wildest dreams
Are but foolish whims, for where she dines tonight,
Is ridden with love not despair.

So let my prayer today be a simple one,
May God enable us to possess a tiny part of her enduring Faith.
We need not look far to find it, it is there in the strum of our hearts,
For God placed emotion at the center of our chest,
Right where Mary could lead us to discover it.

MY FATHER'S HOUSE

PREFACE

Jesus said, "In My Father's house are many mansions; if it were not so, I would have told you. I go to prepare a place for you." John 14:2 (NKJV)

Our perception of God as a Father is filtered through an earthly existence. Some of us had a good example—some poor. The day my father died; I am convinced he left to start construction of his heavenly home. A place where we all can live. The mission for his children, whom he left behind, is to remain focused on the Truth.

How wonderful it will be to work alongside him again.

MY FATHER'S HOUSE

Last night I stood outside my father's house,
Dark curtain sky filled with pinhole lights,
The frozen air cracked with hard work,
I knew he was near.

Leather smell of boots toiled and rough,
Whine of blades, the sawdust swirls,
Marveling at the labor of his hands,
His voice grew bright in my ear.

I felt the warmth of his breath,
Clear like dew on summer grass,
The winter night shuddered at his laugh,
As the vision came all so clear.

Arms raised to the heavens, he stood in ageless youth,
Eyes blue-crystal filled with delight,
The eyes I knew as a child,
Those days we walked the forest path.

Through the iron of heaven's gate,
His voice lifted like a swell in my throat,
I could feel his thought upon me,
Knew his love place a thumb to my heart.

Count the stars in the eastern sky, he said,
Then the west, the north, at last south,
Watch the flowers bloom and fade the day,
Follow the composer as he circles his wand.

MY FATHER'S HOUSE

In the eyes of the unknowing,
Eternity looms lonely as the horizon,
A wave on the endless ocean,
Wandering lost along a serpentine trail.

But I tell you I have seen the Truth,
The Light has stripped away the darkness,
My struggle there was but a dream,
Looking back I marvel at the inconsequence.

Furrowed with valleys the earth takes prisoners,
Listen with your heart, see with your soul,
Find the mountaintops and spy down the abyss,
Watchful of the steps slick with ice.

Constant as the rising sun,
Solemn as the morning forest,
Unwavering as a river bent on the sea, he was,
And I ran, his son, from his ways.

Yet now I see his eyes in my mirror,
I hear his words in my voice,
He is in me, and I in him,
Strangely more the same.

Last night I stood outside my father's house,
Heard the echo of my sorrow fade,
Then with a flutter I felt a throb in my heart,
That I knew he left for me.

NEW LEAF

PREFACE

When I was young, my older brother was an enigma. I knew so little about him. Then he came home from college, and my perception of him became even more puzzling. He was a Jesus Freak. I didn't know what that meant, but that was how he was categorized.

It wasn't until later in my life when I figured out being a Jesus Freak was a good thing. At the time I wrote this poem, I was in the middle of my second divorce, and he was getting married. He too had been through divorce, and I could see how happy he was. Maybe I was hoping for happiness again myself.

NEW LEAF

As the branches of a tree,
These lives become entwined,
Bony fingers against the forces,
Twisted and shaken in the mind.

Bark flayed naked and left to curl,
Torn from the chest and arm,
Nerves of alder exposed and dark,
Caught in a December storm.

A ray of light from a distant sun,
Warming cold the blood congealed,
Leaves borne of spectral energy,
Mere essence love, strong as steel.

A life renewed in summer heat,
Colors vivid dance and carouse,
Oh how the sunlight flickers in her hair,
Blue eyes crystal grace her smile.

Let there grow a canopy here,
A tent of green where you can lay,
Fresh grass abound to prop your heads,
Cool shade cast blue upon the day.

Words can make the heart sing,
Or bring a country to its knees,
Those spoken without contemplation,
Are as vaporous as the breeze.

Let your vows then become as sword and shield,
Growing feverish in the soul,
True eyes open, bright as embers,
As the leaf, the world unfolds.

NEWBORN SON

PREFACE

And Jesus came and spoke to them, saying, "All authority has been given to Me in heaven and on earth. Go therefore and make disciples of all the nations, baptizing them in the name of the Father and of the Son and of the Holy Spirit …" Matthew 28: 18-19 (NKJV)

Baptism is a physical act with dynamic spiritual ramifications. To be submerged in water is a typical occurrence in our daily lives, but when done in the name of the Father, the Son, and the Holy Spirit, a spiritual transformation takes place. A spiritual cleansing that the tarnish of sin cannot mar. A spiritual tattoo the sharp-edged tongue of criticism cannot remove.

NEWBORN SON

In my torturous thoughts
Knives wielded by warriors from the past
I forget the truth, and dwell on demons
Yet like a river, Your spirit flows through me
Eyes welled in pain, red as torn flesh
You have seen more than enough
Yet You say, "Place a finger in My wound,
Never doubt that I am real."

For Your love is the strength of nations
Your omniscience a scalpel refined
With each incision You flay the fearful skin
Stripping away the chains that bind my esteem
Lifting my countenance to shoulder the weight
In Your grace, my heart, an eagle soars
In my faith I find a foothold to rise up
You've pulled me from the quicksand,
plucked a thorn from the earth.

Hence I will no longer doubt Your existence
Nor wonder at my purpose, Lord
For through You I can forge eternity
So find me Lord in prayer
Call my name out loud in the dark
Point Your mighty finger to guide me
Laying my heart wide open for all the world to see
Praying in my nakedness, You have given life,
Your newborn son.

ON BEING TEN

PREFACE

At that time the disciples came to Jesus, saying, "Who then is greatest in the kingdom of heaven?" Then Jesus called a little child to Him, set him in the midst of them, and said, "Assuredly, I say to you, unless you are converted and become as little children, you will by no means enter the kingdom of heaven. Therefore whoever humbles himself as this little child is the greatest in the kingdom of heaven. Whoever receives one little child like this in My name receives Me." Matthew 18: 1-5 (NKJV)

I cherish every moment I have with my son, even to this day, for when he was young, I saw him only every other weekend. That is only 14% of the time. That is the scourge of divorce.

He is twenty-nine years old now, but as I re-read this poem, the innocence of that day struck me, and my heart melted in my chest, for when was the last time I came to my Heavenly Father as if I were ten.

ON BEING TEN

How much fun it was to be down along the creek,
Throwing rocks and watching them disappear
In the lush, or tumble back to earth
From the mossy wall.

To hear the wonderful laughs that he
Would make at each unpredictable fall,
Bounce and splash, joyous eruption
From deep inside his life.

Prodding the newt in the leaves
Along the creek bed, with a stick,
Wondering where his mother was and how cold
His life must be with bugs and rotting leaves
For a bed.

Traveling back to the old rock house, investigating
The cave scribbled with graffiti, scared
By the rubber-winged bat that hangs over the door.

After being at church and reading Proverbs, then off
To NW 23rd, past the horse barns he knew so well
Playing I Spy from the Pizzicato window,
Eating gelato and smelling candles,
Inventing lives for those on the street,
Mysterious black-headed league in the arched window
High above the sidewalk, dressed in black, waiting in black,
Discussions in black.

Throwing rocks at the famous Austin snag—the one
He hit the year before with a mighty bark-chipping blow,
Sending the spider with the white-squiggle-down-its-back
Toward shelter in the arms of a bush.

The size of his hands,
The firmness in his stance,
The sweat atop his forehead,
The color of straw in his hair,
The smell of shampoo lingering there.

It was a perfect day.

OVER THE SUN

PREFACE

Then I returned, and I saw vanity under the sun: Ecclesiastes 4:7 (NKJV)

Moreover I saw under the sun: In the place of judgment, Wickedness was there; And in the place of righteousness, Iniquity was there. Ecclesiastes 3:16 (NKJV)

It is easy sometimes to be dismayed under the sun; seeing the vanity, wickedness and iniquity that exist in the world. However, over the sun lies heaven and my words can only attempt to describe what we will find there for eternity.

OVER THE SUN

Under the sun, there is nothing new.
Season, the grist mill of life, turns endlessly
Upon itself, Orion rises each night in the southern sky
So great a distance that no hand can attain it, then
Squeezes into a pencil-thin line, erased by the horizon.

Rivers flow into a bottomless sea, salted and brined
With a thirst that will never be quenched, Nor the wind
To be tamed for it blows where it wants and the weathervane
Is useless to predict, only react to what has already passed,
Bringing destruction, or cool and inviting pleasure at its whim.

Men toil for meaning and purpose and grasp the vapor
Of their lives, expecting substance as the sand of time
Runs through their fingers, and covers their feet and knees
Eventually covering their remembrance of former things, nor
Will they be remembered by those who come after.

All is futile and vanity, for the eye is not satisfied with seeing
nor the ear with hearing, nor the tongue with speaking, and even
Our necks betray us with a carnal touch while our minds
Make excuses, and the muscles grow stiff to the truth, sodden,
Bending over at the zenith under a weight, not ours to carry.

Over the sun, all things are new.
Time ceases to exist, and the monotony of life subdues
To our imagination as we travel between the stars, Orion
A rest stop on the way to Alpha Centauri, where lunch awaits
Standing atop the horizon, peering over into the accumulation.

Springs of water will flow out of rocks, clear and renewing,
Thirst a character only read about in books, and bridled wind
A chariot of six white horses, snorting and pawing at the ground
Nostrils flaring, the impending charge, as if Hurricane and Tornado
Form sinew and bone, Sirocco and Maria gently holding the reins.

Walking in the coolness of the day, the stillness will be deafening,
Men holding destiny and instruction in their left, gifts and ability
in their right,
And what runs through their fingers will be blessing and
grace and mercy,
Covering their feet and knees until eventually engulfing
everyone around them
With community and love and a gentle
spirit that will never be forgotten.

In that place, futility and vanity become an enigma, joy is the
only dimension,
Hope will satisfy our eyes, future will saturate our ears, the tongue
will be a sword
Of encouragement that will slay all fears, and even our necks that
had been reddened
Under a brutal sun will be allayed, lifting our countenance to the
Lord, friends to speak
Old tales, as Martha and Mary, John and Peter did when He walked
in their presence.

RACE DAY

PREFACE

In 2003, my wife and I visited a church in Puyallup, Washington, seeking healing for her genetic eye disease. The pastor and his wife, Brian and Kristi, were very gracious and prayed for her before the evening service. They were very prophetic, and as they prayed, I had this overwhelming urge to run—run away from there as fast as I could. I didn't know until later that it was the spirit of Pharmakeia that I carried who was eager to get away. A spirit affiliated with drug use, sorcery and witchcraft.

I kept my feelings quiet because I knew my wife wanted to stay, and it was for her we had come. During the service that followed our prayer time, I sat amazed at how young the congregation was—four hundred strong—and they were on fire for the Lord. Some appeared physically disabled, others carried private wounds, I surmised, but I had never seen worship with such intensity.

When the service was over, Brian asked if he could pray for me. I immediately refused. A lame excuse followed. "I'm good," I said. "I don't need prayer." However, he insisted, and for the next two-and-a-half hours Brian, and his wife, prayed over me in front of the altar, and cast out demons one by one until they came to Pharmakeia. It was as though they knew everything about me, and I had never met them before.

By this time, exhaustion had set in, but I still wasn't free. Pharmakeia would not go easily. So, they called over their associate pastors, Matt and Laura, and asked them to finish the job. I remember I was standing, and they put their hands on my chest and prayed with such ferocity, something broke inside me and I fell back into a chair, sweating and spent.

Brian and Kristi announced the spirt had left. Later, I was told that Matt and Laura had never put their hands on me. Yet, something had touched me, and I know now it was the Holy Spirit.

Siting in the chair, I looked toward the front row of the church and saw a woman in her thirties. She had a pleasant face, and she smiled at me. I went berserk. I felt frantic and started yelling for someone to tell me who this person was. Even though she kept smiling at me, I wanted her to leave. I was adamant. I wanted her gone. She was fifteen feet away, like she couldn't come closer, but I wanted her removed.

Brian calmly explained that the woman was a witch. Pharmakeia was looking directly at me, her pleasant face fixed with a ubiquitous smile.

I was unconsolable, so Matt escorted her to the door, while Brian explained her husband was a member of their church, but she had gone the way of Satan. They just ignored her because she had no power there.

When we got to our hotel room, I sat down and in a matter of minutes, I composed the poem that follows. The next day, everything was different. For years, I hadn't abused drugs, but my addictive nature nagged me and was always in the dark of my mind. Now everything had changed. Even the physical world was brighter and more appealing. Deliverance from the control of Pharmakeia and witchcraft had swept the tormenting thoughts away and changed my life forever.

When we got back to Oregon, I emailed Brian the poem and thanked him again for my deliverance. Three weeks later, we went back to the church and during worship; they were singing a new song. A powerful song. A song that sounded familiar, but I didn't realize until afterwards, when Brian told me, the song was the poem. They had written a song based on the poem I had sent and recorded it on their next album. I was told the song eventually made its way into over 400 churches.

This is a long preface to the poem and music that follows, but I felt the context of the events that produced these words, and the evening that changed my life, needed clarity to undo speculation.

RACE DAY

Death and destruction grew from my back as a tree,
Rooted in the bitterness that welled inside me,
Its weight hunching me over in sorrow and self-pity,
Muscles ridged with fear, the bark that enveloped my soul.

The vile harvest, its rotten fruit littered the plain of my existence,
My neck was stiff with inadequacy, the cold touch of
the devil's hand,
He thrived on my weakness, stripped my heart naked
with his cunning,
Left an anvil of sin crushing down upon my shoulders.

He sent his minions to shout in my face,
Their lies licking at my ears,
Feel the curve of the concubine hip, they'd say,
Taste the sweet forgiveness of alcohol and pills.

Fruit of lust, fruit of anger, fruit of rebellion,
Feeding on the poison that cumulates in the soil,
I cursed myself, the only thing I could do well was sin,
Embracing the deception, like a child holds onto a mother's arm.

Athletic potential deprived of a finish line,
Marriage driven to the dead-ends of divorce,
Intellect succumbed to the power of Pharmakeia,
While despair raged in my chest, for I knew not who I was.

Somehow Truth found me no matter where I hid
Persistent in love, He wanted me for His own,
Gaining a foothold in His promise, I wanted to run the race,
But my legs had atrophied in the darkness.

RACE DAY

He carried the burden of my sin—past, present, future,
As I healed, gently guiding me up the pinnacle to forgiveness,
I approached with anticipation, enthusiasm, apprehension,
A journey down a path that evaporates behind my step.

Can there be such a place for me?
Where barriers are destroyed, bewilderment leads to joy,
Though dark forces tried to mire me in confusion,
I wanted to fight for my freedom.

In this place, they came bludgeoned by humanity,
As me, their torsos once twisted in the smoke of hell fires,
Standing tall like wheat four hundred acres strong,
Their heads facing the heavens to soak in His reign.

I clasped my wife's hand, the love she has for me,
As we stood beside each other in this earthquake of passion,
Younger than I, but stronger still, their joy surged through
us and around us,
Such extravagance for the King I had never seen.

Runners were gathering at the gun, athletes trained in praise,
Awaiting the percussion of angels to begin their marathon of Truth,
Race Day—the Lord welling out from this place of worship,
So prolific, the earth to be enveloped in His glory.

And from the thunder came the two for Christ
"Time to lace up your shoes for Jesus," they said,
Sent from above to secure the way,
The steel of my commitment to be forged.

They were the instruments of His love,
The probe and scalpel he would use to search my heart, my soul,
To flay away the festering sickness, and tear
At the roots of bitterness that bound my purpose.

Humility was their strength, Faith their shield,
Wisdom imparted from God to journey into the core
of my mortality,
Releasing me, one by one, from the demons of my life, my death,
Love for a stranger without reservation, warm as the morning sun.

As demons scattered like cockroaches in the Light
Shaking from the battle, my body bent, a reed of exhaustion,
Witchcraft and paranoia caved my legs, heaved and
writhed under my skin,
Fearing the final judgment, they fought on with impudence.

The two brought in specialists to massage my heart,
Pump God's lifeblood back into my veins,
Their ferocious calls on the Lord, powerful and decisive,
Finally breaking the last vestige of the demons' hold.

Then it was done, God had severed the ties
To generation, to death and destruction,
The tree fell from my back unceremoniously,
As I lifted my head to a new horizon.

Today standing in the sun of my Father's love,
Surrounded by the gifts that flow from His grace,
I feel illuminated, eradicated, redeemed in His name,
For if the Lord is with me who can be against me.

Jesus was the first to run the race, made man
He fought the demons' shout unto the cross to save me,
So how much shall I endure to return Him that love?
I know now never as much as He deserves.

Forever I will remember this day of blessing,
Those people who in God toppled the tree from my back,
And I will run the race, no matter the distance,
For it's Race Day—relentless unto the finish line.

Race Day Music

```
G#m7                        F#
```
We've been called to the broken
```
G#m7                        F#
```
To pray Your kingdom would come
```
G#m7                        F#
```
To tear down forces and systems
```
G#m7                        F#
```
Set up by the enemy's schemes
```
E/G#                        F#
```
His poison and lies infiltrated the world
```
E/G#                        F#
```
Offering comfort in the sickness of sin
```
E/G#                        F#
```
But You have called us out as defenders
```
E/G#                        F#
```
And so our heads we raise to soak in Your reign

```
B           G#m7       F#
```
Here we stand at the gun, poised and ready to run
```
B           G#m7       F#
```
Arm in arm surge ahead, trained in batle we're led.
```
E                          F#
```
By the King of kings and the Lord of lords
```
E                          F#
```
He has raised the gun fired to start the run
```
B      G#m7  F#     B     G#m7  F#
```
It is race day,   it is race day

Race Day Music cont.

G#m7   F#
Instruments of Your mercy
G#m7   F#
Equipped with love and your tears
G#m7   F#
Wisdom imparted from your throne
G#m7   F#
We know there's no good within
E/G#   F#
Your words of authority strike down our foe
E/G#   F#
And Your power breaks every hold
E/G#   F#
And the broken ones stand up for Jesus
E/G#   F#
And sign their name to join in on the race
E/G#   F#

Now we're surrounded by those You have chosen
E/G#   F#
Other broken ones set free from their sin
E/G#   F#
So we stand with our hearts full of passion
E/G#   F#
And run this race already knowing we'll win

REMEMBER HOW I WEEP

PREFACE

After my parents died, the glue that held us together as a family dissolved and there became a rift between siblings. Something that I thought indelibly concrete had broken into pieces. It made me ponder the future, the past, and all those things I held dear, wondering when my picture would fade away.

REMEMBER HOW I WEEP

Remember how I weep, for
We are from the same womb,
My father's sperm, my mother's egg.
My eyes wring out the tears, my chest
Heaves with regret.

My mouth sours with disgust, for
We let so many things stand in the way,
We let so many perceptions rob us.
We fell, cheated and slighted and blame
Invades us.

We wrap ourselves in useless idolatry, spending
Our lives in positions without windows,
Not seeing but thinking we see, not hearing
But thinking we hear, not feeling
Just thinking we feel.

No matter how I try I am dying, day by day,
Waiting patiently for falter to begin.
I grow old now and cannot force the way,
I have not the energy I had as a child;
The endless energy.

It came. My joints are frozen. My legs are weak.
My heart struggles in my chest. I am old.
I worked so hard all those years, to achieve,
Yet my bones are frail, my skin loose and dry
About my neck.

REMEMBER HOW I WEEP

My hands don't always do as my mind intends, for
The gears are turning, the secondhand ticks,
But the stem is broken; only my spirit is intact.
I am who toil made me to be, and I will die,
But as He intended?

All my love will not keep me alive.
All my exercise will not keep me awake.
I will perish this body of mine, my work unfinished
My wife without her new coat, my children without
The latest car.

Generations will pass, my picture will be filed away,
My voice has evaporated, my touch gone cold.
They will not know how my hair smelled after a shower
Nor how my smile pulls up at the corner
Of my mouth.

The house I live in will be in ruins, the job
I performed forgotten, to the world
My insignificance will roar, the acquired things,
The amassed wealth, the titles and talent,
Squandered for sure.

No matter how hard I tried, my kids,
My wife felt only imperfect love from me.
What am I for? What am I not?
Christ made me with purpose in mind, I fear
I have fallen.

Eventually time will wipe the slate clean.
Only love and God's promise of redemption
For those who believe will remain; therefore
I need to focus, I need to prepare, before my picture
Too fades away.

SANCTUARY HEART

PREFACE

I grew up in a Catholic home and symbols of the Most Sacred Heart of Jesus were commonplace.

As a child, it was confusing since I didn't know anyone who had their heart outside their chest, but now I know it is a devotion or ritual of worship performed in the Catholic Church. I still have the statue above in my office.

I am not one for worshipping statues, but God's heart is our sanctuary. Just as our heart is the emotional, moral, and spiritual core of a person, God's heart is the source of love, compassion, and wisdom that only He can supply.

SANCTUARY HEART

When the breath escapes you,
When the void chill of night
Settles deep into your bones,
Lay hold of the Sanctuary Heart,
For in its gold lies the strength to go on.

When infirmity plagues you,
When words spoken callously,
Cut layers through your skin,
Lay hold of the Sanctuary Heart
For in its shape lies the love to go on.

When darkness circles 'round you,
When the looming past closes in,
To rob you of the glories ahead,
Lay hold on the Sanctuary Heart,
For in its spirit lies the forgiveness to go on.

When the future scares you,
When the weight of the world,
Crushes down upon your shoulders,
Lay hold of the Sanctuary heart,
For in your Father lies the answer to go on.

SILENCE

PREFACE

We were traveling the day when our friend Mark suddenly died. He fell to the floor in front of his wife, Laura, an aneurism in his brain rendering him helpless to survive.

I remember I was driving while so many thoughts flooded my mind. I am not sure how other people handle life when it makes little sense, but I write. It is my way of putting all the pieces back in order.

I gave Laura these words, hoping that they might console her loss, and lift the burden of sorrow that came suddenly to cloak her life.

SILENCE

As if a teacup suddenly tipped over my life
Ceramic blue surrounds me; I feel Laura's hand
On my neck, her breath on my cheek
Her love for me more precious than life itself
Seasoned and strong as staves of oak.

In my mind's eye a white stallion is jumping, charging
Against the gate with nostrils flared, chest heaving
Clouds of baited smoke as the grip of imperfection
Loosens, slipping like a rope through the hands of those
Whose halter and bit tried to contain me.

My chest is stirring with God's Holy Spirit, undeniably so
For I have felt Him before and He me, in times
Of struggle and praise and laughter and sorrow
Sometimes at arms length beyond my grasp
Where I relinquished Him in my weakness.

Yet now peace is tangible as flesh, smooth as milk
My heart scarlet red caught in a kaleidoscope
Of emotion that never diminishes, but turns
Over and over upon itself in new ways of brilliance
And color that renders in the coolness of green.

I saw in her eyes the panic of departure, her love
Tugging at my shirt to stay, her lips forming
The words she never wanted to say as thoughts
Foreign to her raced in tortured circles, tightening
While the world went static around us.

I could not speak, but I had so much to say.
I could not move, but I had so much to embrace.
Yet at that moment, welling up from deep inside
Beyond the poet's words, the silence was broken
By the shouts of angels storytelling of our love.

Do not pine for me, nor fret what should have been
For when you feel the cool breeze on your face, or taste
A bold sweetness in your mouth, or hear the sound
Of the meadowlark call, that is I who still reveres you;
That is I who has gone to build a mansion for us to live.

THIS LIFE ESCAPES ME

PREFACE

As with the poem *Center of My Desire*, this poem was born at an Alpha retreat in Rockaway Beach, when I would get up early Saturday morning to find a place to sit and wait for the Lord to speak.

This poem proves to me that God is always close. We can see Him everywhere if we just take a moment to look and really see.

THIS LIFE ESCAPES ME

The sun is finally breaking,
Driving out the last tears from the sky,
While orange hues of morning,
Break across the crown of trees.
The colors radiate Your glory,
There is solace in this place.
I hear the waves crashing white on the rocks,
As the struggle of men surround me,
Yet here I find Your love and peace,
Feel the whispery wind of angels' wings.
For I am home in Your presence, unfettered
Sensing with each breath, this life escapes me.

TO KNOW LOVE

PREFACE

There are many types of love, but the love for a spouse is the oldest love besides God's love for us. He created that love in the Garden of Eden, allowing man and woman to be one flesh.

It is a special love, born out of tribulation and trust, forged in the fire of life, strong enough to cross the chasm between death and eternity.

TO KNOW LOVE

Bleeding the page
Hope and sorrow mingle red
To be all to one, a dream
Heaven sent in angel's arms.

Twist as smoke
Roots grasp the passion earth
Harden oak to stand the storm
Shade the grass blue, cool day.

To know love past the cordon life
Last breath sweet as cherry
Visions painted on a canvas soul
Carry me forever.

TOMORROW'S GOLD

PREFACE

The night I wrote this started with me loading up the front seat of my 1974 Ford pickup with a few belongings and driving away from my home. It was January 1999. My second marriage was over. I had nowhere to go, but I knew I couldn't stay there.

I pulled over alongside the road and called my good friend for advice. He told me to go to his house and move in. He was in Cabo San Lucas, and he told me to take care of his house until he got home.

I was alone. My children were not with me. I was at an intense, low point in my life. When I got to my friend's house, it was dark and cold, and I sat with my back to the wall and cried, the ambient light from the world outside streaming in over my shoulder. I picked up a pen and paper and wrote these words.

TOMORROW'S GOLD

Have you ever been on a drunken weep
Where life is short and emotions sweet
Strong cord heart, mind of courage
Feelings scarred
Deep as a river, clear as a shout
Tear my paper skin hands of the roiling tide
What was is no more, what is to be
Flashes gold tomorrow
Slivers to my eye, staves to my soul
Loneliness intense calls the gathering gloom as insects to the feast
I am but a myth unto myself
A wish to soar into the spectral light.

UNDER A SHELTERED SKY

PREFACE

God's love for us is undeserving, and I do not believe we would know how to love each other if He hadn't authored it from the beginning. My love for my wife may seem endless, but without Him, love would simply not exist.

UNDER A SHELTERED SKY

Under a sheltered sky
We as children lay our heads
Embraced in a wrap of comfort
Caught in a time-spun web.

For in God's fervent touch
True blessings brought ten-fold
He graced us with his favorite gift
A wonder ancient, never old.

Sure deep is the eternal ocean
Wide is the crescent universe
Vast is thy fruitful imagination
Immortal is the spoken verse.

Yet cast in the balance of fortune
Weighed against this godsend true
All shrink empty into cold oblivion
Compared to my love of you.

WORD

PREFACE

My father wrote his memoir before his death in 2002. My mother finished hers in 2007. I am very appreciative that both took the time to write their memoirs, allowing me to have a permanent record of their life, but also providing valuable insights into who they were as my parents.

I know the Bible isn't a memoir. However, just as my parents left me writings that serve as an anchor to my past, I appreciate God leaving His scriptures to serve as a guidepost to my future.

WORD

I can imagine my Father
Standing on a ridge, in the forest,
His suspenders taut on his shoulders,
Smell of wood smoke rubbed into his skin.
Though, save for the steel blue of his eyes,
The features of his face have run from my memory.

Together the sound of his voice, which I'd known from birth,
Has since death also faded from my cells, yet today
His words are as clear as the mountain stream
He so enjoyed, and their meaning in my life
As strong as the hands that gripped an axe at fourteen.

I can imagine as well, my heavenly Father
Sitting on a throne, in an olive grove,
Mankind a leather yoke about his shoulders,
Smell of ancient myrrh rubbed into his skin.
Though, save for the steel Truth of his eyes,
The features of his face are unimportant to me.

The sound of His voice has never graced my ears,
Though His thoughts appear in my mind sometimes
Without volume, or accent, as a voice might,
As clear as if I had said them myself, yet
With sure wisdom I could never muster.

My father wrote some words for me to read,
Of history, and family, and heritage; portraits
Of struggle and might, humility and aggravation,
They are in my eyes a testimony of courage,
A collection that reconstructed the man.

God, our Father, wrote His Word for us to read,
Of beginnings, and toil, and endings; portraits
Of sin and sacrifice, prophesy and truth,
They are in my eyes authority over darkness,
A collection that deconstructs mankind.

YELLOW BRICK ROAD

PREFACE

I wrote this poem for my good friend Ron, who had been battling cancer for many years. I am sure sometimes he felt done and out, but I never saw it. He had brains, heart and courage, and the ruby slippers of humor. Everything he needed to guide him to his heavenly home. The Emerald City may be magnificent, but there is no place like home when that place is called heaven.

YELLOW BRICK ROAD

A lesser man would have stayed with the Munchkins
Instead of venturing out into the woods, where trees
Pitch apples and witches fly on brooms.

In a land of make believe he could have been Mayor, safe
In his goatee, high collar trench coat, figurehead of
The Lollypop League, sporting Dippity-do hair and curl-toe shoes.

A lesser man would have told the Tin Man, straight-up
"Your heart is an organ with no spiritual value," save
For poets, and lyricists, and schoolgirls with becoming smiles.

To the Scarecrow, his hat stitched tight to his head, lighten-up
"Knowledge is over-rated. God loves the weak," true
Or not, you'll see, ignorance placates the feeble-minded.

A lesser man would have told the Lion sure, buck-up
"Courage is for those who have no future," sacrifice
Will make a fool, as you, seem utterly noble indeed.

Then Dorothy, sweet Dorothy, naïve and chaste, listen-up
"Hope is sparkly and crimson like ruby slippers," sold
As a pair at auction, bows included, for thirty pieces of sliver.

A lesser man examines a speck while standing firmly
On his plank, unaware that he is everything that he affirms
Not to be, blindfolded, his pirate's sword tipped at his back.

On his journey to the Emerald City and ultimately
To Oz, he would've grown cynical, suspicious, a Tin Man
Hollow, his heart two-times-too-small for his chest.

He would have found himself bright and intellectual,
Straw-minded, taking to the bricks with calculation, a Scarecrow
On fire, engulfed in his own reasoning and delight.

Undoubtedly, he would have avoided the woods, too
Dark and dingy, a dismal place for social illiterates, a Lion
Bold, would venture not, while unwittingly losing his way.

To be humble or meek, that is just not wise, a servant
Full of hope, a lesser man to argue, is ridiculous to pursue,
A juxtaposition of terms, as upside-down as right and wrong.

Not this man. Not this time. Not now. Not ever.
If steadfast was a tree, he'd be a mighty oak, if
Faithful was a jewel, he'd be a sea of diamond.

One cannot quantify the amount of blessedness
In a man, nor weigh his Spirit on a scale, as if such
Had dimension or mass, or elements of time.

Only in some other realm, caught in an hourglass of Truth
Squeezing from one universe to the next like shimmering
Gold through the portal of heaven, do they exist.

 A lesser man would have focused on his hands, his horizon,
Pleasure and position, a trove of inconsistencies and chance,
Summed up as luck or a candy cane of fate.

Not this man. Enduring hammers of choice, pendulums
Of Hope, future vaporous as smoke, he senses the hourglass
Finding consolation in the order of the sand.

His name means powerful. His name means wise counsel.
His love is boundless. His humor endless. His prominence
Revealed by the One he loves, not the toil of his hands.

This man sees the unseen and knows it is real, this man
Finds stature in association with a King, this man knows
Where his strength comes from, this man.

YOUR GLORY

PREFACE

As with the poem *Center of My Desire*, this poem was born at an Alpha retreat in Rockaway Beach, when I would get up early Saturday morning to find a place to visit and wait for the Lord to speak.

Close to my cabin was a jumble of logs tossed there like matchsticks. I remember standing on a giant nurse log, the moss thick along its trunk, and once again the Lord did not fail me.

YOUR GLORY

I have been waiting, waiting LORD
My eyes are filled with the wetness of your glory
You guide me by still waters
See your angels turning in the mist
Gathering over the water
Rounding about You in praise
As the sun rises above the tree line
The ancient giant tree which has fallen
Nursing new life for so many,
Just as the giants of old
Help nurse us along

What does yonder bird proclaim?
The glory of the LORD

www.ingramcontent.com/pod-product-compliance
Lightning Source LLC
Chambersburg PA
CBHW060331260626
47160CB00007B/2769